THE ABSOLUTELY, POSITIVELY, DEFINITELY FINAL

GOOD NEWS BAD NEWS

By MARTIN A. RAGAWAY   Illustrations by DON ROBB

a *Laughter Library* book

PRICE/STERN/SLOAN

Publishers, Inc., Los Angeles

1984

Copyright© 1984 by the Laughter Library
Published by Price/Stern/Sloan Publishers, Inc.
410 North La Cienega Boulevard, Los Angeles, California 90048

Printed in the United States of America. All rights reserved. No part of this publication may be reproduced, stored in a retrieval system, or transmitted, in any form or by any means, electronic, mechanical, photocopying, recording, or otherwise, without the prior written permission of the publishers.

ISBN: 0-8431-0989-0

Good News: The railroad has a deal where you can go anyplace in the U.S. for $200.

Bad news: You have to go by Amtrak.

Good news: I found out last night that my wife is turned on by leather.

Bad news: She opened an account at Gucci's.

Good news: **The President is doing the best he knows how.**

Bad news: **The President is doing the best he knows how.**

Sergeant: The good news is that Private Hargrave, who weighs 350 pounds, will set the pace for our 10 mile run. The bad news is that Private Hargrave will be driving a truck.

Bad news: My husband fell asleep at the wheel of his car last night.

Good news: It was a drive-in movie.

Waiter to Diner:

Bad news:

All we have today is fresh octopus.

Good news:

We just sold the last portion.

Landlord to Tenant:

Bad news: The border has been changed and your house is now in Poland.

Good news: You won't have to go through another one of those terrible Russian winters.

Good news: Your wife decided not to run off with her lover.

Bad news: *Your girlfriend did*

Good news: Your heart transplant operation was a complete success.

Bad news: They gave you back your old heart by mistake.

Good news: My daughter managed to catch the bouquet in church Sunday.

Bad news: We were at a funeral.

Good news: *I got God to reduce his 101 commandments to just 10.*

Bad news: *The one on adultery is still in there.*

Bad news: The unemployment insurance lines are getting longer and longer.

More bad news: By the time you get to the counter, you'll qualify for Social Security — but there won't be anything left.

Good news:
I spotted the first robin of spring.

Bad news:
He spotted me first.

First the good news: Your painting is a genuine Peregrini, who worked with Leonardo da Vinci during the Renaissance.

Now the bad news: Peregrini was Leonardo da Vinci's plumber.

Government official to businessman:

Good news: I was sent out here by Washington to help you.

Bad news: I was sent out here by Washington to help you.

Bad news: A 14 ton satellite is falling on New York.

Good news: It'll be stripped clean before it hits the street.

Insurance Broker to 91-year-old Rabbi

The good news is that I was able to get you malpractice insurance so you can continue doing circumcisions

...the bad news is the insurance company is insisting on a two inch deductible.

Minister to Congregation:
The good news is that God created the world in six days and rested on the seventh. The bad news: we're in this much trouble because God only put in a six day week.

Bad news: Your brother fell out of the upper stands at Dodger Stadium.

Good news: The shortstop caught him on one bounce.

Bad news: Your new girlfriend won't do anything without her mother.

Good news: Her mother does everything

Movie producer:

Good News: We're making Jaws 5 in which the shark attacks Beverly Hills.

Bad News: The story is the same but the shark wears braces.

BAD NEWS: Your wife has become a nudist.
GOOD NEWS: She's out shopping for nothing to wear.

Good news: Your brother was seen on tv when he became the one-millionth person to enter the First National Bank.

Bad news: He's in jail. The bank wasn't open yet.

Good news: According to a survey, college girls prefer to go to bed with middle-aged men.

Bad news: According to the survey, they consider middle age as 32.

Good news: Your car is not one of those being recalled by Detroit.

Bad news: Since it's Japanese, it's being recalled to Tokyo.

Good news of the future:

Good news: "Congratulations, you're the first black family to settle on the Moon."

Bad news: "Until we work it out, your kids will be bussed to downtown Mars."

Good news: The stork dropped a bundle on your doorstep.

Bad news: It's not a baby. You'll have to take your pooper scooper and clean it up yourself.

Good news: According to the divorce settlement, your wife gets the kids, the house and the car, but you have visitation rights.

Bad news: Once a week you get to see the house and the car.

Bad news: I just found out my wife is a secret shoplifter.

Good news: Everything she's brought home so far fits me.

Good news: Your Holiness, I've just received word that Jesus is coming back to earth.

Bad news: He wants us to meet him in Salt Lake City.

Good news: Your thirty year mortgage will be paid off.

Bad news: Now that the house is falling apart, it's all yours.

Good news: I've finally discovered the Fountain of Youth.

Bad news: At my age, I've forgotten what I wanted to do with it.

Good news: While you were gone, your little boy fed the goldfish.

Bad news: He fed them to the cat.

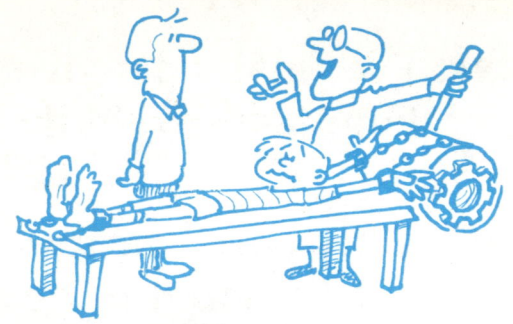

Good news: We put your son on a stretching rack and he's grown an inch.

Bad news: He's confessed to 43 crimes.

Airline captain to passengers:

Bad news: "We're in the middle of the ocean, past the point of no return and we're almost out of gas."

Good news: "Those in the back can come up front and die in first class."

Fortune teller to client:

Bad news: You'll be poor, unhappy and miserable until you are forty years old.

Good news: By that time you'll be used to it.

Good news: My wife just presented me with a beautiful blue-eyed blonde-haired baby.

Bad news: I'm an Eskimo.

Iranian official to the Ayotollah:
"Your holiness, I have good news and bad news. The good news is that you've been elected President."

"And the bad news?"
"You've been elected President for life."

Good news: "What turns you on? Are you a breast man or a leg man?"

Bad news: "We're sending out for fried chicken."

Good news: *Mr. President, the Soviet Premier is calling on the red phone to say he's in favor of free speech.*

Bad news: *He reversed the charges.*

Good news: **Now that your baldheaded daughter's taking hormone shots, she has hair down to her ankles.**

Bad news: **It starts at her knees.**

Good news:

Your wife is keeping a cat around the house so she won't be lonely when you travel.

Bad news:

This cat is 6 foot 8 and plays basketball for the Celtics.

Good news: My youngest son is already potty trained.

Bad news: My youngest son is 27-years-old.

Good news:

People are less selfish and are sharing things more than ever before.

Bad news:

This announcement comes to you from the National Institute for Herpes.

Good news: **In our socialist country, medical care is free so your abortion will be absolutely free.**

Bad news: **There's a two-year wait.**

Bad news: **Your wife just ran**
Good news: **That knocks two**

Good news: Your grandfather's
been in the family
Bad news:

Good news: ☼ Solar power will
cars and factories.

Bad news: The

off with your best friend
eople off your Christmas list.

will left you something that's
or years.

t's your grandmother.

soon provide energy for homes,

rabs now own the sun.

Distraught father:

The bad news:
My teen age daughter is in Central America devoting her life to wiping ugliness off the face of the earth.

The good news: So far she's gotten rid of two pimples and a zit.

Captain of the Titanic:

Bad news: Ladies and Gentlemen, I'm sorry to report we've run into an iceberg and the ship is sinking.

Good news: The bartender was almost out of ice.

Good news: Issac Newton was sitting under a tree when an apple fell on his head. As a result, he discovered the law of gravity.

Bad news:

He also discovered the migraine headache.

Letter from Bessarabia—
Your long lost uncle died:
The good news: You've inherited 500,000 gherkins.

The bad news: Gherkins are little pickles.

Dentist to Patient:

"I have *good news* and *bad news*. First, the *bad news*. Your teeth are in rotten condition. I'll need to see you two hours a day for six months and it will cost you at least $15,000."

"What's the *good news*?"

"I just bought another apartment house."

Good news: Miss Anderson, we've finally found a way to make the office less crowded.

Bad news: You're fired.

Bad news: I regret to tell you that your Van Gogh was not painted by Van Gogh

Good news: It was painted by Picasso.

Good news: A fantastic girl invited me for dinner and asked me to pick up a couple of cans of Alpo.

Bad news: She doesn't have a dog!

Good news: A Norwegian penny, dated 1,000 A.D., was discovered in Maine which proves the Vikings discovered America.

Bad news: The Vikings were also lousy tippers.

Postmaster General to Media:

"The good news is that the post office is going to reduce postage rates to 10 cents an ounce. The bad news is it's no longer based on how heavy your letter is but how much your mailman weighs."

Letter from the Public Library:

The bad news is that the six books you took out are overdue. Worse news: So, is the librarian.

Good news:
Men...today, you get a change of underwear...

Bad news: Pulaski, you change with Masseroni...Masseroni, you change with Goldberg...Goldberg, you...

Pilot to Co-Pilot:

Bad news: We've lost power on all four jets and the plane is going down.

Good news: The movie sucks.

Navigator to Submarine Commander:

Good news:

We made the emergency dive, Captain, and we're down to 500 feet.

Bad news:

The water is only 400 feet deep.

Stewardess to Pilot:

Bad news: We have a hijacker aboard the New York to Miami flight

Good news: He wants to go to Miami.

Bad news: My wife's been kidnapped and they're demanding $100,000 or I'll never see her again.

Good news: There's no way I can get my hands on $100,000.

Good news: That old painting that you found is a Rembrandt and has been appraised at $1,000,000.....

Bad news: It and the appraiser are missing.

Good news: Your car was the only one on the block that didn't get a parking ticket. **Bad news:** It was towed away.

The good news is that you've won a million dollars in the Publisher's Clearing House contest.
The bad news: Your money is coming by U.S. Mail.

Fortune Teller to U.S. Senator:

First the good news:

You will be nominated for the Presidency of the United States.

Now the bad news:

You will win!

Good news: A child psychologist has stopped my child from sucking his thumb by putting soap on it.

Bad news: Now he goes around sucking soap.

THE GOOD NEWS IS

You're definitely not sterile.

You're going to have a new disease named after you.

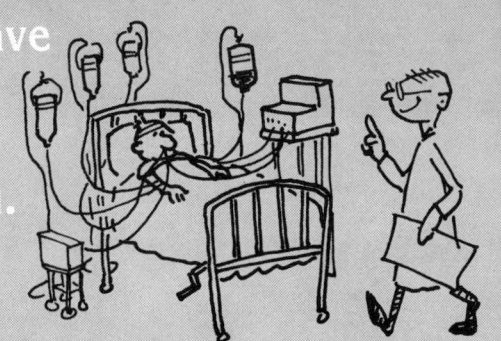

The right front fenders and the trunk won't need any work at all.

THE BAD NEWS

The door and the ice cube trays do not have to be replaced.

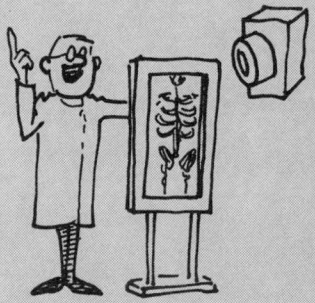

You're not a hypochondrias.

Out of our seven children, six did not break their arms today.

Gynecologist: I've got good news and bad news. Your vibrator is stuck and I can't get it out.

Patient: What could the good news be?

Gynecologist: I was able to change the batteries.

Good news: Your wife took a photo which could be worth $50,000.

Bad news: It's a picture of you and your girlfriend coming out of a motel.

Real Estate Broker to Home Buyer: The bad news is that your mortgage payments on your 40 year loan are $1200 a month, every month. The good news is that you get to spread it out over this century and the 21st.

Good news:
Your horse came in first in the sixth.

Bad news:
He was running in the fifth.

Scientist: *The bad news is that smoking pot can cause a man to develop female breasts. The good news is that it's cutting down on sexual harassment at the office.*

Good news: Gold has been discovered on the Johnson ranch.

Bad news: It was Harry Gold and he discovered fooling around with Johnson's wife.

Good news: "I called this guy who owes me a thousa bucks and he told me the check is in the mail."

Bad news: "It was a recorded announcement."

Good news: *At the next port, there will be food and grog for everyone.*

Bad news: *The Captain wants to go water skiing*

Bad news: Your Dodge Colt drove off the ridge into the Grand Canyon...

Good News: It got 37 miles to the gallon on the way down.

Bad news: I got arrested for speeding and reckless driving.

Good news: My teenage son is giving me more respect.

Good news: Your daughter got on the scale today and found she'd lost 14 pounds.

Bad News: She was arrested on a 703 – taking off her clothes in a drug store.

Apostle at The Last Supper:

> "I have some good new and some bad news. the good news is that we have the honor of being at this special dinner with Jesus. The bad news is: those on the other side of the table won't be in the picture."

Pilot to passsengers:

This is your...hic...pilot...

First, I'll give you the...hic...good news. We're circling at twelve feet...

Bad News:
We're still inside the hanger.

Bad news: The weather forecast for tomorrow is for five degrees below zero.

Good news: I got your air conditioner fixed.

Good news: **Tests prove that vinegar definitely gets rid of kitchen odor.**

Bad news: **Nothing gets rid of the smell of vinegar.**

Good news: You've made the Olympic javelin team.

Bad news: How good are you at catching javelins?

I have some good news and some bad news...In this test tube there are all the male chromosomes...and this jar holds all the female chromosomes... when I pour the test tube into the jar, I will create life.

Now, the bad news...we can't do it tonight because the jar has a headache...

Bad news: A meteorite falls on your house.

Good news: You own it.

Good news: Your son just broke the Olympic record for the triple somersault from the high board.

Bad news: He broke everything else.

First the good news: *I'm here to inform you that you've won the New York State lottery... one million dollars...*

Now the bad news: *I'm with the Internal Revenue Service...*

Good news: *Ladies and Gentlemen, this is your Captain speaking...we have lost power on all four jet engines but we are not in any danger...to lighten the load, some members of the crew have put on parachutes and bailed out.*

Bad news: *This is a recording.*

Good news: Our Uncle George went on an Africa safari and we now have a stuffed lion in our den

Bad news: It's stuffed with Uncle George.

Good news: Professor, you're nominated for a Nobel Prize for discovering a cure for hermophodosis.

Bad news: There's no such disease as hermophodosis.

Bad news: My daughter married a homosexual

Good news: He's a doctor.

Fortune teller to lady on other side of crystal ball:

Bad news: Your husband will be murdered.

Good news: You'll be acquitted.

The Good News is that we feel guilty about only paying $24 for Manhattan, so we have decided to give it back to the Indians.

UGH!

NY DEED

The Bad News is they refused it.

This is a

a *Laughter Library* book

published by

PRICE/STERN/SLOAN
Publishers, Inc., Los Angeles

Other Laughter Library titles include
the following "2 in 1" books

**THINGS YOU DON'T WANT TO HEAR IN THE HOSPITAL/
THINGS TO THINK ABOUT WHILE WAITING FOR YOUR BEDPAN ($1.95)
THE NICE THING ABOUT LIVING ALONE/
THE TOUGH THING ABOUT LIVING ALONG ($1.95)**

and

**WHAT DO YOU GET WHEN YOU CROSS . . . ($1.75)
BETS YOU CAN'T LOSE ($1.75)
FISHING FOR LAUGHS ($1.75)
FUNNIEST FOOTBALL STORIES OF THE CENTURY ($1.75)
FUNNIEST BASEBALL STORIES OF THE CENTURY ($1.75)
X-RATED RIDDLES ($1.75)
HOW TO GET YOUR TEENAGER TO RUN AWAY FROM HOME ($1.75)
HOW TO KEEP THE KIDS FROM MOVING BACK IN! ($1.75)
GUILT WITHOUT SEX ($1.75)
FUNNIEST RIDDLES OF THE CENTURY ($1.75)
SEX BEFORE GOLF ($1.75)
FIRST THE ANSWER...THEN THE QUESTION ($1.75)
YOU KNOW YOU'RE OFF YOUR DIET WHEN ($1.75)
THE BEVERLY HILLS PRINCESS ($1.75)
YOU DON'T HAVE TO COUNT YOUR BIRTHDAYS UNTIL . . . ($1.75)**

For a free list of P/S/S titles, send us your name and address.

The above Laughter Library titles and many others can be bought at your local bookstore, or can be ordered directly from the publisher. Send your check or money order for the total amount plus $1.00 for handling and mailing to:

DIRECT MAIL SALES

PRICE/STERN/SLOAN *Publishers, Inc.*
410 North La Cienega Boulevard, Los Angeles, California 90048